Witchcraft for Beginners

A Guide to Bringing Real Witchcraft Spells and Witchcraft Rituals into Your Daily Life

Table of Content

Summary

Introduction

Chapter 1: History of Witchcraft

Chapter 2: Witches, Witchcraft & Magic

What is a Witch?

What is Witchcraft?

What Is Magic?

Chapter 3: How To become a Witch

Difference Between White Witchcraft And Black Witchcraft

Common Types of Witchcraft

How To Become a Witch

Beginner Steps

Chapter 4: How To Practise Witchcraft

The Do's And Don'ts Of Practising Witchcraft

Chapter 5: Spells for Beginners

Chapter 6: Conclusion

Summary

Thank you for taking your precious time to read this book. I am so excited for the knowledge that you are going to gain by reading this book. I hope you will revel in every single page of this book and you will be able to apply every bit of knowledge present inside into your life. Enjoy the read!

When most individuals think of witchcraft they usually picture a very old unpleasant, lump-ridden women clad in black robes, soaring over a cauldron that contains a mysterious, bubbly potion while chanting an incantation in a bizarre form of speech. Or possibly you may also easily think of the contemporary Hollywood imageries of young witches as sensual teenagers in gothic apparel and black lipstick, wearing huge silver pentacles, having unbearable attitudes.

However in truth neither of these images accurately portrays witchcraft or witches especially since witchcraft has absolutely nothing to do with what a person looks like or what they wear and has lot more to do with how someone lives the craft in life. In a practical sense there definitely may be old lump-infested women who perform witchcraft and there may also be arrogant attractive teens who practice witchcraft. But this does not at all show the depth and knowledge that is in Witchraft that is waiting to be attained by the student of this knowledge.

With this book you will acquire all the knowledge you wish to have if you have ever even remotely thought about practicing witchcraft. From the introduction, you will learn the true in depth meaning of the basic term witch and also learn the practice of real witchcraft itself. Apart from that you will receive an overview of the history of witchcraft and you will definitely understand why over time it has come to be associated with darkness and evil.

As you progress in the book you will also have exclusive knowledge on how to easily start off witchcraft spells and rituals as a beginner. There is a great selection of easy beginner spells detailed for you in the text that you can easily integrate into your life and slowly by slowly bring some real magic into your life.

Introduction

Witches have been existing in every single society of the global domain since the primordial times. They have always been linked with performance of magical spells. However, the role of a witch went past the realm of magic only. Witches used to be the community's doctor, who cured the patients with herbs, chants, potions, oils , stones, oils, massages, and of course, the rituals and magic. The magic consisted of using wands, going into trances, getting in touch with ancestral spirits and reading of omens. Witches were also capable of interpreting voices, visions and dreams that their patients saw at night or even during the day.

Today you can be a witch irrespective of the religion that you are in. You can become a witch and still be a Christian, Muslim Jew, Buddhist, Hindu or even an atheist.

Highly respected men and women in society especially those with advanced levels of education proudly proclaim themselves as witches. In the United States of America alone, there are thousands of them. In fact their tribe is on the rise in terms of numbers as times goes by and the same is also happening in a variety of other countries of Canada, Australia and Europe. This is because of the wide and all- inclusive nature of the practice of witchcraft that gives each and every individual a chance to follow their own intuitions and instincts

In simple terms witchcraft could possibly be the most autonomous creed in the world that agrees to maximum freedom for every practitioner of the craft, both in thought and in action. There is no control of thought in the practice of witchcraft. You are not obliged to adhere to the doctrines of any particular faith or tradition. You can even come up with your own chants, spells, rituals and circles or even just the way you worship. You can choose to join a coven or just practice it by yourself

Majority of the witches make use of the Book of Shadows as their point of reference and a guide for their witchcraft practice. This enables them to preserve their capabilities with the spells, chants rituals and magic that they find useful to them and to the lives of others.

Chapter 1: History of Witchcraft

In the ancient times, Witchcraft was a knowledge that was full of mysteries. Every single piece of information, including the cuisine recipes of our grandmothers, which are vital for our living, is rather mysterious even in the present day. Most of this information is similar to business secrets today, which cannot be divulged to just any individual. In that case the witches only passed on their information to close relatives and those they loved. It was therefore a normal trend for witchcraft to be inherited by the children from their mothers and their grandmothers.

Witches loved and cherished Mother Nature and they also worshipped nature in all its expressions. They deeply respected and admired the earth, trees, planets, animals, sun, moon, stars, clouds, rain, rivers, lakes and even the oceans. Witches felt enlightened and impressed at the ever changing forms and the moods of Nature and they regarded them as the forerunners of change, whether positive or negative.

Witches used to have a deep knowledge of the profits of herbs, plants and trees. For instance, they had distinctive admiration for the oak tree and it was considered sanctified. The Mistletoe, a parasite that grows on the oak tree was also considered to be a valuable herb. This herb was used for healing purposes and in rituals and ceremonies. Usually, it was harvested during the Summer Solstice with the use of a golden sickle. The moment it was chopped off, it was gathered on a piece of cloth in order to stop it from making contact with the ground when falling.

Just like any other type of knowledge, a number of witches in the olden days used their skill in the craft for evil designs for instance by use of hexes and brooms. Despite the evil doing by the minority, the practice of witchcraft was largely used for charitable and caring purposes.

But then since evil deeds have the tendency of attracting much more attention than the decent, moral and respectable deeds, witchcraft was all of a sudden considered a knowledge that was evil. This was the case especially by the most influential individuals in the society in those days and the by the high priests of the Church.

Sooner than later a typical witch was then depicted as an ominous looking elderly woman that wields a broomstick and performing acts that were well thought-out to be evil by both the society and the church. For that reason, even the Scottish Witchcraft Act of 1563 penalised even the individuals who were directly linked with witches or those who sought their help in solving their medicinal problems.

From then on, younger individuals avoided the practicing of witchcraft especially out of the fear of torment, discrimination and the general persecution by both the society and the church. Those who kept going on with their practice slowly aged and became ugly especially as a result of complete poverty, fear of persecution and scarcity of basic needs as time gradually passed. Some of them even had to live most of their lives in hiding. It is mostly for these reasons why witches have been majorly shown to be wart-ridden, old, fearful, ugly and mean.

Fortunately, with the coming in of the New Age the practice of witchcraft has progressively regained its ancient respect. In fact in the present day, witchcraft is being extensively practiced by people who are widely educated.

Chapter 2: Witches, Witchcraft & Magic

What is a Witch?

The word witch derives its origin from an Anglo-Saxon word 'Wicca'. Again, this word 'Wicca' is a derivation of the word' wicce' which is used to mean 'wise' According to majority of the definitions today, a witch is a magician, a female sorcerer or an enchantress. In the present day a witch is also defined as a believer in Wicca or a Wiccan

What is Witchcraft?

As the name indicates, this is a 'craft' that is practised by witches. It is mainly referred to as witchcraft and not wizard craft since in the ancient times women are the ones who ordinarily practiced it. So in a way, witch craft is usually associated with women.

It was mostly practiced by women also because women used to stay at home whereas the men went out to fend for the family back at home. These women provided help to the people of their community particularly the women in curing of diseases.

In addition, Witchcraft was also commonly referred to as the 'The Craft of the Wise.'" It was given this name since its practitioners used to live close to Mother Nature and were able to cure diseases in the community, which was a service that no one else could offer. For the reason that witches stayed very closely connected to Mother Nature, over a period of time, they gained the ability to decipher the healing properties of a variety of plants and herbs.

Slowly, as already indicated, the practice of witchcraft was faced with the consequences of time and it started being well-thought-out to be evil. In history there are quite a number of times when women were mercilessly burnt to the stake for the practice of witchcraft. This was mainly as a result of superstition.

In point of fact witchcraft is not a religion, it basically is a 'craft'. Witches generally follow a religion known as Wicca. Therefore, because the beliefs or rather the basic principles of witchcraft are also followed in Wicca, the practice of witchcraft is largely identified with religion.

Witches perform their crafts either when they are alone or in their own sacred groups known as covens. The key benefit of practicing by yourself is that you have the ability to initiate yourself into witchcraft alone and begin your practise immediately. You are not obliged to wait for the individuals in a particular coven to initiate you into the craft.

The major advantage that comes with working in a coven is that you will have an opportunity to learn quite a lot from the experience and understanding of the other members of the coven. In addition, a united worship in a group tends to evoke much more powerful magic or energy as compared to individual worship.

Witches realize the power and strength of rituals, worship and prayer and they specifically use them for problem solving in their society. They have been doing this for a long time and they still keep doing so in the present day. For instance, they recognize the power and strength of positive affirmations and chants that are habitually used in the course of praying. The moment these affirmations and chants are used with total focus and concentration, they acquire some very powerful energy.

During the performance of worship a special kind of conducive environment is created. This could be done with, for instance, incense and burnt fragrant candles, drawing of circles while uttering chants and performing rituals. All the combined impact of the mentioned practices works like magic.

What Is Magic?

A lot of individuals struggle with the proper definition of this term. Some consider magic to be pure spiritual power, whereas others consider it to be just as equally a force in the natural world as electricity or even gravity. One of the most popular beliefs is that magic doesn't really violate the natural physical laws of the universe, but it is purely a law by itself which we have not yet had the scientific understanding that fully explains it.

Similar beliefs are held about psychic powers and other supernatural phenomena. In this standpoint, magic is quite similar to dark matter. We know it is in existence, but we just cannot fully explain what it is or how it looks. Witchcraft is the usage of magic in order to achieve an end that cannot be easily accomplished through normal means.

Chapter 3: How To become a Witch

In simple terms, witchcraft is a tool that enables you to release the inner power that is within you. We all have this inner power and it is upon us to choose where exactly we want to take this power; whether it is to a good place, or a bad place.

Difference Between White Witchcraft And Black Witchcraft

Similar to the way any specific apparatus, tool or instrument can be used for good or for evil, witchcraft can also be used the same way. Unluckily, this is one of the major reasons why witchcraft received a lot of bad reputation over the years. Too many individuals have used the practice to fulfil their not so honourable desires for power, greed and lust. Despite the evil reputation witchcraft can be used in helping to heal disease, attract wealth and even buoy up fertility. In fact, it can also be used to build up your relationships and grow your self-confidence.

The major difference that comes between the practice of white witchcraft and black witchcraft is basically the intent that lies behind the practitioner. The moment witchcraft is used to bring harm and adversity to other individuals, or even just to wield your control over other people, that is black witchcraft. On the other hand, if you use it to bring joyfulness, pleasure, prosperity, love and well-being into your own life, and the lives of other individuals, then it is regarded as white witchcraft.

Common Types of Witchcraft:

The following are the most common types of Witchcraft;

•Hedge Witchcraft – witchcraft that is based on nature, bringing out elements of astral projection as well as health-giving, shamanism and midwifery

•Electic Witchcraft - A merger of a variety of traditions which includes but is not entirely limited to the traditions of witchcraft

•Green Witchcraft – Witchcraft that is mainly focused on the elements of nature such as earth

•Kitchen Witchcraft - Applied witchcraft that focuses on the use of natural specimen common to everyday livelihood such as herbs

•Gardnerian Witchcraft - The continuance of the witchcraft that was practiced by the inductees of the founder of Wicca, Gerald Gardner.

•Neopagan Witchcraft – Characteristically, this is the practice of witchcraft in the service of one's own ancestral divinities

How To Become a Witch

There are actually no specific covert initiations and rites of passage that one must undergo in order to become a witch. Basically, you just need to turn to your inside and start acquiring knowledge about your very own spiritual or psychic power, and how to effectively make use of it. This therefore means that you are required to, improve your concentration, harness you own mental ability and learn how to elevate your own energy and discharge it in the direction of the creating a particular outcome. It seems rather complicated but it is actually not.

You can just start by thinking about the last time you needed something so much. How you kept constantly thinking about it. How you always fantasised about it, how you kept praying for it, and eventually took action to bring it into your life. Witchcraft also uses an identical process of mindful intent, focus and taking action in order to make an opening for the new state of affairs to come into our lives. Therefore, the practice of witchcraft is basically making effort to learn how to tie together and then focus the spiritual and mental power which you already have.

A large number of the experts of witchcraft make use of scented oil, incense, herbs and candles among a wide range of other witchcraft related objects. Still, it is quite significant for you to understand that these objects are just props. These are not necessarily needed in order to practice witchcraft. These objects simply provide a focal point, which enables you to let out the power that is within yourself.

Beginner Steps

The most important steps for you as a beginner to take in order to integrate witchcraft into your life are;

- Read and learn.

There is quite a lot of vital information present in this book that will easily enable your practice of witchcraft take off. However, this craft is very wide, therefore, you can get even more knowledge by getting out of your comfort zone. Pay a visit your local public library or even just the New Age section of the bookstore within your locality. Start looking through the volumes existing on the practice of witchcraft. You will get quite a number of ideal collections to pick out from. A part from that, there are also a wide range of helpful websites with information that will be quite useful. Just perform random searches on, the internet and explore the many available options. Nonetheless, it is imperative to remember that there exists lot of witchcraft interpretations out there. A number of them are good and some of them are not very good, while others are absolutely dangerous. Thus, it is of importance for you to trust your own inner instincts over any witchcraft material that you come across. The moment something starts feeling even remotely bad or wrong, you have to let it go. You should only retain the information that feels factual deep within yourself. This way, you will be able to stay on the right path which will enable you to make decisions that are of benefit to you

- Daily meditation.

You should make a habit of simply spending five to ten minutes every single day quietly sitting and make an effort to get in touch with your own centre of spirituality. Focus on draining your mind of all thoughts and connect with the tranquil silence that is inside you. This will take exercise, especially as your thoughts will probably scatter because as a beginner you do not yet have a resilient level of intellectual concentration. However, with constant practice, day in day out, it gets a little easier. Sooner than later you will have the ability to use and channel your power of concentration in any practice of witchcraft that you perform.

Chapter 4: How to Practise Witchcraft

Before you even begin casting a spell, you have to spend some substantial amount of time doing some research for the specific witchcraft you are about to practice. There are a variety of forms of witchcraft, and the one that best reverberates with you is the one which determines exactly how you cast a spell. You should learn as much as possible about the variety of traditions and then look for physical symbols of invisible forces or qualities, also referred to as correspondences that appeal the most to you

There are a wide range of Spell-craft Tools and Witchcraft Supplies that you require in order for you to have the ability of casting a spell. Some of the most commonly used include;

- Cauldron - A small-sized pot which is normally moulded with the use of cast iron, it is used in mixing and heating up of potions and concoctions for spell-work.
- Athame - A blade that is used for casting a protection circle for spell-work, it is also used in the course of spells

- Mortar & Pestle - A small-sized cup which is usually also moulded out of cast iron, with a blunted crushing and grinding tool. It is used in the crushing of spices and herbs for rituals and spells

- Wand - A piece of wood, a stick or any other material that is used in the casting of a circle

- Magical Talismans and Amulets – These are very powerful symbols which can be used in spell-craft. They are also worn for magical enhancement and daily protection.

- Herbs - An assortment of both easily available and uncommon herbs are used for augmentation of effect to portions and rituals; one of the most commonly used herbs for purification and protection spells is sage.

- Flowers –A wide variety of spells call for the addition of flowers in their preparation since they have powerful symbolic meanings and their more obvious property; stunning fragrances

- Statues of God & Goddess – They are used in the drawing of focus to the God and Goddess in the course of rituals. These may also be used to call upon their manifestation to a circle of a ritual.

- Gemstones – Each and every gemstone used in the practice of witchcraft has magical significance, and can therefore be used as a communication channel in rituals or in healing spells
- Crystals - These are commonly used in the purification of a consecrated space preceding a ritual, hence providing protection and healing. Crystals also are used as a means of amplification of the magical characteristics of the gemstones
- Salt –The element that is normally used in the casting of a protection circle, prevention of evil spirits from gaining access to a room, and a variety of other protective and cleansing spells.

Some of the above mentioned items could cost you a significant amount of money whereas some barely have a price. But then, most of these items are very cheap.

A very powerful witchcraft spell or ritual can be accomplished without even spending a dime. You can simply go to your desired nature spot, for instance the woods or a beach and collect some stones, dirt shells, feathers, leaves, sand animal bones, seeds or even fossils; as long as an item has some magical significance to you. These items will not cost you anything but still hold the same power in spell-craft as compared to the pricey counterparts that can be found online.

Important Note; Despite the fact that all the above mentioned items can be used as vital correspondences for spell-work, in order for you to cast a spell you actually do not need any specific physical item. The practice of witchcraft tends to majorly draw its power and strength from the intents and will of the user. The correspondences or tools are items of power that can be employed in drawing focus and symbolizing the strength and power that is within yourself and within Mother Nature.

The Do's And Don'ts Of Practising Witchcraft

As a beginner of the practice of witchcraft, you can follow the simple ritual outline below;

- Cleanse the Area.
- Prepare the Altar (it does not have to be too ostentatious, just a few of your favourite tools e.g. You can just light a candle)
- Cast the circle.
- Welcome the elements.
- Invite the Divinities.
- State the purpose of the ritual.
- Devote your magical working
- Raise the energy and then release it
- Ground.
- Thank the Deities.
- Thank the elements.
- Close the circle. (also referred to as opening the circle)

There are a variety of other easier or even more intricate ways of performing a ritual. Most traditions tend to have their own formats. However, if you learn and understand how to do this straightforward ritual, you will be at ease in any open Circle that you may decide to take part in.

a) Begin with the first step of the above list. You can make some short hand notes on every step in your journal as you start planning your ritual. Choose how you will cleanse your working area. You can either do it with a besom/broom, salt and water or incense. You should also choose what you will place on your altar. (Compiling a list first assures that you won't forget anything, such as the matches to light up a candle.)

b) Before you begin, take your time to silently sit and centre yourself. Be truthful about your emotions, feelings and thoughts. If you are either feeling anxious, scared or excited, just know that that is a normal feeling. This is very important and therefore should not be taken lightly.

c) Talk to your ancestors about what you are about to practice. Despite the fact that they already know what you are about to practice and they are willing to help, it will be comforting for you to say this in case you end up having the feeling that you may have done something in a way it is not supposed to be done. Have confidence and always remember that you are "practicing" and this essentially involves some amount of trial and error. There is no one above laughing at what you are doing.

d) Slowly and carefully perform each and every indicated step. Give the symbols an opportunity to speak within you. Take a moment in between every step and feel the effect the ritual has had on you and your surroundings. In the course of grounding, pin your ears back for answers...pay attention to advice...hang on to yourself...take note of your surroundings for instance, a ringing phone that you dint remember to take off the hook....

e) Keep listening. Usually, we have the tendency of asking for things and then we fail to take the time to pin our ears back for the answers. You should take short hand notes of everything and doodle impressions on the margin section of your note book. The symbols you doodle could later be of importance.

f) Keep repeating this exact straight forward ritual over and over again. You will probably realize that it becomes more significant every time that you practice it. The child within your subconscious mind will be definitely enjoy it

The Don'ts

i. Never worry about whatever you are going to say. You should always say what is deep inside your heart. Make use of very simple language and do not forget to take deep breaths in between the sentences you are speaking. Your intention is to alter your consciousness and not entirely losing it!

ii. Do not take any pledges or make life time commitments to the Deities. At this point, it is still too early to make that decision yet. You are still in the discovery process trying to find out if Witchcraft is truly your right path. Taking oaths is among the most vital decisions that you will ever make in your life. You should therefore give it the reflection and respect that it deserves.

iii. Do not be afraid. You are probably nervous as a result of all the Hollywood movies you may have watched about the start of an actual ritual practice. You should know that nothing like that is going to happen. As long as you have made sure that you have done every step bit by bit and with much consideration you do not have to keep worrying. The only way situations can get unpleasant is only when you make an effort to go into places for which you are unprepared for.

iv. Do not practice your witchcraft ritual for a very long time. Also, you should not practice the ritual too often. You should instead come up with a regular schedule for instance once every week and make sure that you stick to that schedule for a while. If you really feel like doing something daily then go for something simple such as a ritual of candle lighting in the morning or evening. Witchcraft is basically grounded on the "rhythms' of Mother Nature, therefore, you should consider performing ritual work on moon phases or holidays for instance.

Chapter 5: Spells for Beginners

Since you are still quite new to witchcraft, you should try beginner spells so that you can start understanding how the spells work. Easy witchcraft spells are one of the best ways to get your feet wet and begin gaining the knowledge of the art of magic. They can still provide impressive results even without any additional trouble.

The moment you find a simple spell that suits your purpose ensure that you put your complete effort into it. Even the simple spells require both your energy and concentration so that they can work. Sometimes simple spells turn out to be the best spells. They may probably not feel quite as magical as an intricate ritual, but then, a lot of witches tend to feel they have the ability to focus more on their intents rather than worry about all the complicated details. Take your time, focus on what you are performing, and have conviction that it is going to work. Below are a few fine spell examples that you can easily practice as a beginner.

1. **Knot Your Troubles**

This one can be used irrespective of the intensity of your troubles. Just choose a colour of the string that suits your purpose. The best way to select the colour is by fine-tuning the spell to your specific circumstances. You can even refer to a magical colour chart for precision if you are not sure. For instance, if you want to banish negativity use a black piece of string

The string should be at least 12 inches long. Now, grasp the string, with one end in every hand and then tighten it with your pull. Think about a single problem per spell. Ponder on your difficult state and begin tying knots in the string. As you do that, visualize all your predicaments getting tied up in the knots and being shut in there. Keep on tying up to the point where you feel it's adequate.

Take the tangled string outside and then bury it to so that you can keep your problems buried far away.

2. Sprinkle of Protection

Requirements

- A trickle of some coarse salt
- A teaspoonful of some garlic powder

DO NOT use with commercial garlic salt! Mix together the salt and garlic, and then evenly sprinkle some of the mixture on each entry point to your household. That simply refers to the doorways, window ledges and even ventilation openings if you can gain access to them. This will be an effective way of keeping out any type of negative energy that may follow you to your house.

3. Two Halves Love Spell

This is a very simple love spell that you can try as a beginner witchcraft practitioner.

Requirements

- 1 white candle
- 1 red candle
- A piece of paper
- a pen

Light up every candle on the altar that you have set up, or even just table as long as it is a place where they will not be disturbed. On the piece of paper, note down the qualities you would like in a love partner. Remember to remain realistic, write a maximum of six things on the list.

Tear the piece of paper into two halves, and then burn the first half in the white candle's flame and the second half in the flame of the red candle. A suitable significant other ought to come into your life soon

4. Health Blessing

The objects that are used in this spell are a representation of vitality and health. They are NOT in any way medical cures for a specific disease.

Requirements

- A glass full of apple juice
- 1 stick of cinnamon
- 1 white candle

You should ensure that you use natural ingredients for best practice of witchcraft. Therefore, make an effort of finding some organic apple juice. Pour the organic apple juice into a glass then stir exactly four times with the cinnamon stick. Light up the white candle and then take a few sips of the juice.

Repeat the following:

> Goddess bless my body and my soul,
> Health and wellness is my goal

Finish the remainder of the juice and then put out the candle. This spell should be performed on every occasion you feel an ailment coming on. You can also perform it each morning for your health and bodily well-being

5. Clear an Argument Spell

Whenever persistent bitterness is keeps you from making up with a cherished comrade, this spell could help in clearing the bad air between you two and renovate the bond of your friendship.

Requirements

- 1 dry bay leaf
- 1 yellow candle
- A small-sized paper envelope

Note down your name on one side of the paper envelope, and the name of your friend on the other side. Put the bay leaf inside the paper envelope and then seal it. Light up the candle and then hold the envelope up in the candle flame until it completely burns up. You can place the burning envelope inside a heat-proof bowl to prevent your fingers from burning up

6. Happiness Candle Spell

This spell can be a quick way of jump stating happiness in your life. It is very simple and it can give you the ability to see things more positively.

Requirements

- Two orange candles
- Dried lavender

Place a few lavender pinches on a prepared altar or just on a table in the middle of the two candles. Light both candles and give your hand a chance feel the warmth of those flames. After that, repeat these lines 7 times:

This spell please bless,

For my happiness.

Let the lit candles burn down completely and you will start having some rushes of happiness in no time.

7. Melting Weight Loss Spell

Most individuals tend not to be contented about their weight. This spell can help you with shedding off that excess weight. However, you have to be completely honest with your inner self about whether you truly have to shed off those extra pounds.

Requirements;

- 1 brown candle

Make a small carving of your current weight at the top of the candle and then carve in your target weight the bottom. You have to be realistic while setting the target. Each single night before you retire to bed, light the candle up for fifteen minutes. As the wax from the candle melts down closer to the target weight, you will start slimming down.

8. Bury and Banish

This spell can be used if you feel you no longer want to be ever involved with someone.

Requirements;

- A black sheet of paper

Write the name of that person in the middle. You do not actually have to be able to read the name, as long as it is there, that is good enough. Fold up the piece of paper to the smallest size possible, take it outside and then put in the ground. Once you burry it, say the following phrases out loud:

Into the ground,

You cannot be found,

You are not around,

I cannot heard your sound,

Step over the place you have buried that piece of paper, and that individual will in a little while fade away from your life.

9. Classic Love Spell

This is among the most commonly sought spells. It contains all the classic elements of a good magic spell. This is performed in order to bring new love into your life.

Requirements;

- 1 pink candle
- Rose oil
- A few dried rose or lavender petals

Evenly scatter the petals around and then and set your candle holder on the top. Take the rose oil and then rub it along the candle. After that, light it in the candle holder. Repeat the following words:

I wish to find love,

I wish it to last,

I wish to find love,

May it come fast.

You need to repeat the words three times, after that you let the candle burn out. From there, you should watch for a new upcoming love into your life.

Just because you are a beginner, you do not have to limit yourself to very simple spells. As you continue with your progressive learning of the witchcraft spells and rituals, you can even try out some of the more intricate spells which require a lot more ingredients. Some of these advanced rituals can only be practiced at certain times of the month, year or in certain natural occurrences such as eclipses. This therefore

means that your timing of the ritual pr?
very important. Here is one spell that requ..
strictly adhere to its period of practice.

10.   The Blue Moon Wish Spell

The "Blue Moon" that appears on the 31st of August is in the horoscopic symbol of Pisces. It illuminates intuition, creativity and compassion. This is the time that you should start thinking about all your wishes and intentions. As a practitioner of witchcraft, you should make sure that you perform this ritual since such an astrological opportunity only occurs "once in a Blue Moon".

Requirements

- a quartz crystal
- a cinnamon stick
- A blue pen
- a blue candle
- a sheet of parchment paper
- 3 safety pins
- a glass of spring water or wine

- A piece silver cord or string, of a length of 24 inches
- a square of blue cloth
- Vial of success potion (not mandatory)
- 1 book of matches

On the day before of the Blue Moon, collect all the above items and then set a specific time for performing the spell without any distractions.

Quietly sit down with all your items as listed above and place them before you on a table. Shut your eyes and bring your mind to silence, after that, concentrate on your breathing. The moment you feel clear and grounded, you can open your eyes and start the spell.

i. While lighting the candle, think of 3 things that you would like to occur by the year's end. You can also wish for something that takes place once in a blue moon. (rarely)

ii. Pat success oil on your, wrists, temple and your neck for a boost in case you have some.

iii. Envision one particular wish coming true, while holding the quartz crystal in your hands. Vision yourself doing the thing you are wishing for, or clearly see something that you wish for happen before you.

iv. Pick your pen and paper up and start writing down your wishes as you keenly visualize them. Note them down in their order of importance to you.

v.   After you note down the three wishes on your piece of parchment, separately tear them out

vi. Attach each of your wishes to the square piece of cloth using a safety pin

vii. Place the cinnamon stick in the middle of the cloth and then inwardly fold the sides of the cloth. After that, roll it up.

viii. Tightly seal your projections by wrapping the string around the cloth nine times and after that, tie steadily with a knot.

ix. Take your wishes and walk outside with them while holding the libation of your choice. Look up to the sky or the moon. Lift up your glass and say the following words;

"On this eve of the Blue Moon,

out my intents go.

I request they be received, and it is so"

Place the cloth containing your wishes in a concealed place where you are the only one who can see it often all the way through the coming few months as a reminder to the wishes you have made.

On the New Year's Eve, you can unfold the cloth and check the number of manifested wishes. If some of the wishes have not yet manifested, you can reassess and then carry out this spell as a projection spell of the New Year's Eve. You will slowly cross things out of your list, as the Universe sorts it all out.

You can also keep carrying the quartz crystal with you in the course of the coming year as a constant reminder if your wishes. You can also take it with you on any significant discussions or meetings for a successful outcome

Chapter 6: Conclusion

As you have already seen, the practice of witchcraft is not as scary, difficult or even as evil as it is always portrayed. In fact, its origin came out of a good place of love, care and responsibility. We all have this power within us and you do not have to have special abilities to practice it. The only thing that is required of you is the readiness and willingness to open your heart, mind and spirit to its possibilities. As a beginner, the spells illustrated in the book are a fine way to start off your practice. The more you practice the better you get at the craft.

That way, you will build a strong foundation from which you will keep growing and building your skill as a witchcraft practitioner. Along the way, you will over and over again pause to think about about new resources and visions. Ensure that you go slow and make an effort to reflect a lot on what meaning these concepts personally bring to your life. It is also crucial to allow the freshly acquired ideas to come to be integrated into your own spirit. That is the only way that they can become "real' in your life and experience as a practitioner of witchcraft. The spells and rituals will start being a part of who you are and will be in harmony with how you feel and think. One of the best ways to enhance your spiritual connection is with constant practice.

Never forget the witchcraft code of conduct that says;

"Mind the Threefold Law you should,

Three times bad and three times good"

This means that the moment you do harm to others with the practice, harm will come to you three times as much. Just like the law of karma. Therefore, whatever you practice, make sure that it does not bring harm to any individual.

You should always bear in mind that learning the practice of witchcraft is a process that will never be complete. There will always be more information to acquire, more procedures to try out, and more knowledge to gain about your inner self. Just focus on taking it one step at a time as each day unfolds and try to learn as much as you can. Consider your progress as a thrilling journey, and you will find yourself enjoying every single moment of it.

Once again, thank you for buying this book and taking your time to read it. Good Luck!

53161152R00027

Made in the USA
Lexington, KY
24 June 2016